# ◫ READERS

## Level 3

# A Note to Parents

DK READERS is a compelling program for beginning readers, designed in conjunction with leading literacy experts, including Dr. Linda Gambrell, Distinguished Professor of Education at Clemson University. Dr. Gambrell has served as President of the National Reading Conference, the College Reading Association, and the International Reading Association.

Beautiful illustrations and superb full-color photographs combine with engaging, easy-to-read stories to offer a fresh approach to each subject in the series. Each DK READER is guaranteed to capture a child's interest while developing his or her reading skills, general knowledge, and love of reading.

The five levels of DK READERS are aimed at different reading abilities, enabling you to choose the books that are exactly right for your child:

**Pre-level 1:** Learning to read
**Level 1:** Beginning to read
**Level 2:** Beginning to read alone
**Level 3:** Reading alone
**Level 4:** Proficient readers

The "normal" age at which a child begins to read can be anywhere from three to eight years old. Adult participation through the lower levels is very helpful for providing encouragement, discussing storylines, and sounding out unfamiliar words.

No matter which level you select, you can be sure that you are helping your child learn to read, then read to learn!

LONDON, NEW YORK, MUNICH,
MELBOURNE, AND DELHI

**Series Editor** Deborah Lock
**U.S. Editor** Shannon Beatty
**Designer** Jemma Westing
**Production Editor** Sean Daly
**Picture Researcher** Rob Nunn
**Jacket Designer** Natalie Godwin
**Natural History Consultant**
Tom Fayle

**Reading Consultant**
Linda Gambrell, Ph.D.

First American Edition, 2011
Published in the United States by
DK Publishing
375 Hudson Street, New York, New York 10014

11 12 13 14 15 10 9 8 7 6 5 4 3 2 1
001-182473-August 2011

Published in Great Britain by Dorling Kindersley Limited.
A catalog record for this book is available
from the Library of Congress.
ISBN: 978-0-7566-8932-2 (paperback)
ISBN:978-0-7566-8933-9 (hardcover)

DK books are available at special discounts when purchased in bulk
for sales promotions, premiums, fund-raising, or educational use.
For details, contact:
DK Publishing Special Markets
375 Hudson Street, New York, New York 10014
SpecialSales@dk.com
Printed and bound in China by L Rex Printing Co., Ltd.

The publisher would like to thank the following for their kind
permission to reproduce their photographs:
a=above, b=below/bottom, c=center, l=left, r=right, t=top
**Alamy Images:** The Africa Image Library 7; Guillermo Lopez
Barrera 23; Stan Gregg 30; JJM Stock Photography 20; H. Lansdown
40; Patrick Lynch 26-27; Jack Thomas 4tr; Christian Ziegler / Danita
Delimont 16. **Corbis:** Michael & Patricia Fogden 14-15; Martin
Gallagher 32-33; Steve Kaufman 21. **FLPA:** Mark Moffett / Minden
Pictures 43; Piotr Naskrecki / Minden Pictures 5crb, 7br, 17b, 38;
Christian Ziegler / Minden Pictures 10-11. **Getty Images:** Gallo
Images / Travel Ink 41tr; National Geographic / Tim Laman 8-9;
Stock Illustration Source / Peter Siu 4-5; Taxi / Hans Christian Heap
37. **naturepl.com:** Mark Bowler 2, 3, 4br, 15cr; Martin Dohrn 5bl;
Kim Taylor 5tr, 12-13, 34bl; John Waters 39. **NHPA / Photoshot:**
Ken Griffiths 46-47; Dave Pinson 42; Dr. Ivan Polunin 36.
**Photolibrary:** Richard Packwood / Oxford Scientific (OSF) 34-35.
**Science Photo Library:** 23tr; Ted Clutter 31; Gregory Dimijian 19;
James H. Robinson 5tl, 28, 29. **SuperStock:** Minden Pictures 11,
17tr. **Alex Wild / myrmecos.net:** 13t, 22, 24bc, 24-25, 44, 45.
**Jacket images: Front:** Nature Picture Library: Meul / ARCO
All other images © Dorling Kindersley
For further information see: www.dkimages.com

Discover more at
**www.dk.com**

# Contents

**DK** READERS

READING
**3**
ALONE

# Ant Antics

Written by Deborah Lock

**DK**

DK Publishing

# Ants alive!

*Carpenter ants: We are found all over the world. Meet us on page 30.*

Ants have been on Earth for more than 110 million years. They've spread out all over the planet and there's an estimated 10,000 trillion of them crawling around.

More than 12,000 different kinds of ants have been named and there are probably many thousands more. They survive by working together in colonies. Each tiny ant busily does a vital job to keep the whole colony going. Find out about the amazing busy lives of six different ants. ❖

*Leafcutter ants: We live in Central and South America. Meet us on page 14.*

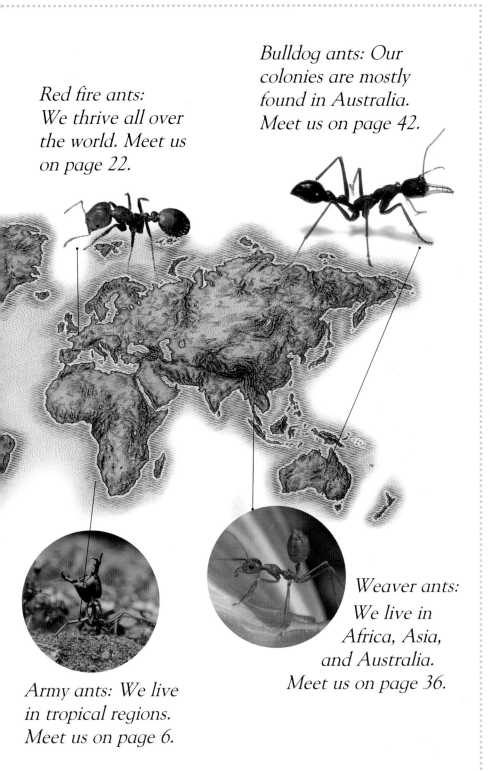

Red fire ants: We thrive all over the world. Meet us on page 22.

Bulldog ants: Our colonies are mostly found in Australia. Meet us on page 42.

Army ants: We live in tropical regions. Meet us on page 6.

Weaver ants: We live in Africa, Asia, and Australia. Meet us on page 36.

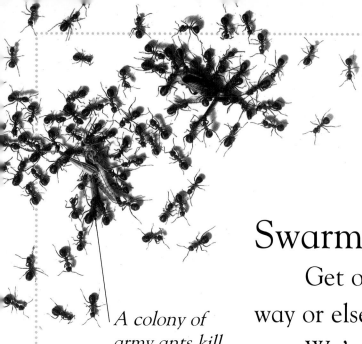

# Swarm raiders

*A colony of army ants kill more than 100,000 animals a day.*

Get out of our way or else!

We're army ants, and we're always on the hunt for food.

If you were a small animal in our path, you'd have no chance against us even if you were bigger than us.

First we'd overwhelm you with our numbers. There are more than 200,000 of us on a raid. Then quick as a flash, we'd cut and slice you into tiny pieces, so that we can carry the pieces back to our nest.

## Ant senses

Ants have poor eyesight but amazing antennae to feel around and pick up smells. Ants use their antennae to find their prey, know where they are, and communicate with each other.

We might be tiny, but it takes us less than 10 minutes to cut up a 2-in (5-cm) long spider and take it away to our nest, leaving nothing where the attack took place. We know our way back to the nest by following the scent trail we leave as we fan out across the forest floor.

Large soldier ants line our trail
and are ready to protect us if we are
attacked. They have much larger
mandibles than us—the worker ants.

mandible

Back at the nest, we hand over the pieces to the smaller workers. They crush the pieces, squeezing out the liquids to feed our queen, the larvae, and the rest of the colony.

Our nest is unusual. Look closely, and you'll notice it's made up of thousands of ants. When we rest we fasten onto each other, using the hooks and spines on our mandibles and on our feet. There could be more than one million ants in one colony.

## Bivouacs

Army ants make living nests called bivouacs. By linking together, they form walls and tunnels, keeping their queen and her 120,000 eggs and young protected.

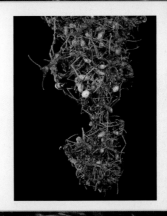

The site of our nest is only temporary. Once we've raided an area and can find no more food, we all move on. We mostly march at night in a long column, protected by the soldiers. We're just like an army. Some workers carry the queen and her eggs, and others carry the larvae.

Some workers go on ahead to
check out the area, leaving a scent
trail for the rest of us to follow.

In the daylight, we set up camp
again, linking together to make
a new nest.

Now we're ready to go
out raiding again.

Quick!

March! ❖

# Fungus farmers

Make way! We're coming through with our heavy load. These pieces of leaves might not look heavy to you, but they're five times our body weight.

We're leafcutter ants and we're all very busy. We are the harvesters, carrying the leaves to our nest. Smaller workers sit on top to stop flies from landing on the leaves.

It takes us several hours to scuttle back and forth from our nest to where the large workers are slicing off the pieces.

These workers cut the leaves with razor-sharp teeth on their mandibles, which vibrate powerfully a thousand times per second.

*Leafcutter ants can carry pieces at least 6 times their body weight, which is the same as a human carrying a small car.*

Once at the nest, we take our pieces underground and hand them over to some other workers. We don't eat the leaves but use them as compost to grow a certain type of fungus. The fungus is our food.

The underground workers grow the fungus by cutting and chewing the leaves into a gooey pulp. Like gardeners, they take great care to spread out the leaf pulp, cover it with our droppings, and then place a small piece of fungus on top.

There are millions of us in the colony and we're all sisters. Our mother, the queen ant, lays thousands of eggs every day. The younger workers look after them.

Our nest covers a large area and has several entrances. Inside, we've dug out hundreds of chambers that are about the size of a soccer ball. We grow the fungus inside these chambers.

We have many enemies such as hunter spiders and other ants. Our large soldiers protect us from these intruders by biting them hard with their mandibles.

*The small, young workers are the nurses, moving and cleaning the eggs and feeding the larvae.*

As you can imagine, we create huge amounts of waste because there are so many of us. Some workers have the very important job of removing all the old fungus and waste. Like garbage collectors, they take the waste and either bury it deep within the nest or pile it up outside. Workers on the heap move it around so that it breaks down into soil quickly.

The rest of us don't go near these workers. We don't want to catch the germs and diseases that may infect the leaves and fungus.

Well, we can't just hang out talking. More leaves are needed. Off we go again! ❖

# Fiery team workers

I wouldn't step on our nest if I were you. You don't want to upset us since we can get very, very angry. And when we're angry, we each use our lethal weapon—a poisoned stinger! We are red fire ants and we can now be found all over the world.

When we attack, we grasp our victim with our mandibles and then arch our backs under our bodies to inject venom from our stinger. We pivot on our heads and sting around in a circle. Our poison can kill small creatures and cause an extreme burning pain in humans, too.

### Sting reaction

Fire ant stings cause painful swelling and blisters and burning itchiness of the skin, which needs treatment. In some cases, people can have a life-threatening allergic reaction.

**Life spans**

An adult male fire ant lives for about four days after leaving the nest. A worker fire ant lives for about 180 days. A queen fire ant can live up to seven years.

Our colony was started by a young queen and a group of worker ants in just one day. She had wings back then and flew off to mate with winged male ants. Since then, our queen has been laying 1,500 eggs a day, which hatch into larvae.

The larvae change into pupae for a few weeks and later become adults. Then these young workers start looking after the queen, the eggs, and the larvae, and keeping the colony clean. Our colony grows quickly. In a year, our colony had 11,000 ants and, after three years, there were 60,000 of us.

You might think we are troublemakers because we infest farmland and hurt you, but we are successful because we are organized and work together as a team.

Older workers risk the dangers to go out and search for food. We eat everything—animals and plants—squeezing out the liquids to suck. Working together, we can attack and kill a lizard in less than a minute.

Many of us stay inside the nest digging out new chambers and tunnels to make room for our growing colony. Sometimes our nests have more than one queen so our colonies can have half a million ants. To make room, we dig deeper and deeper. Some of our nests can be 5-ft (1.5-m) deep.

We push the soil up to the surface, leaving mounds more than 3-ft (1-m) high above the ground. Quite an achievement for tiny creatures! So please, don't step on us. Be impressed and keep your distance. ❖

*A red fire ant has a darker abdomen than the rest of its body.*

# Wood tunnellers

We don't eat wood. That's the truth! We just use our mandibles to break it up to make tunnels and chambers for our nest. We are carpenter ants and we make nests for our queen in moist wood. Her eggs need moisture so that they don't dry out. Most of us live outside in rotting trees, roots, and logs.

### Nest sites

Indoors, the nests of carpenter ants can be found in damp or hollow places, such as around sinks, showers, and dishwashers, under roofs, and in doors and walls.

Ok, we're guilty! We do venture indoors and can do terrible damage to your homes and other buildings. Also as our colony grows, we make other nests for just the workers and larvae in other wooden boards or beams.

*As they nest and tunnel out the wood, a large colony of carpenter ants may be heard rustling or gnawing.*

We're attracted into your homes by the sweet-tasting foods you have. Honey, jelly, and sugar are our favorites. Outside, we find little insects called aphids, which ooze out sweet honeydew when we stroke them. We also feed on other insects, cutting them into small pieces and squeezing them for the juices.

Like all ants, we have two
stomachs one for our own food supply
and another for food to regurgitate
(bring back up) and share with the
colony. We're most active during
the spring and summer, going out
at night to forage for food to bring
back to the nest.

In late summer, workers try to collect more food so that many of the larvae can be well fed. These well fed larvae develop into winged queen and male ants. The following spring, when the weather is warm and humid after rain, the winged ants fly from the nest. They travel far and wide. Winged ants from other nests do this at the same time.

In great swarms, the queens mate with the male ants. Afterward, the male ants die and the queens find suitable damp homes for their new colonies. I'll bet you're hoping this will not be indoors! ❖

# Weaving wonders

Hold on! Pull! Nearly there! Pull! We're weaver ants and the most amazing thing about us is how we make our impressive treetop nests.

Have you ever tried sewing together a bag? Well, you take a piece of material—in our case, that's a leaf—and then fold it over, so that the edges can be sewn together. There needs to be many, many workers for us to do this.

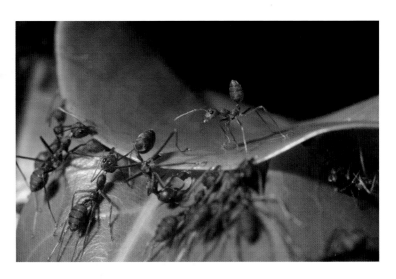

We line up along an edge of a leaf and hold it very tightly in our mandibles. Then we begin to bend the leaf edge over toward the other edge. More workers join us, linking to our feet and helping us to pull until the edges are nearly touching.

Then, yet more workers bring larvae from our old nest and gently squeeze them. Oozing out from each larva comes a thin thread of silk. We then work on sticking the edges of the leaf together, using the silk.

Our nests can be very large, as we then begin connecting another leaf and then another. Sometimes our nests connect branches from two trees. Impressed?

We don't damage the tree. In fact, we protect it since we stop other animals from coming to live in the tree or eating parts of it.

We have many enemies that try to trick us, though. Some caterpillars produce sweet liquid called honeydew, which we love to eat. While we are distracted eating the honeydew, they crawl into the nest to eat our larvae.

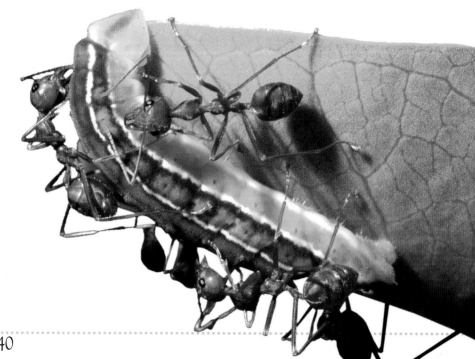

*Jumping spiders don't make webs but stealthily hunt for their food.*

Jumping spiders smell like us, so they are able to enter our nest undetected to eat the eggs, larvae, and us. It's tough being an ant! ❖

# Speedy hunters

We can see you! Unlike other kinds of ants, we have large eyes and excellent sight. We are bulldog ants and we are one of the largest kinds. We are as aggressive as wasps. In fact, scientists believe ants are close relatives of bees and wasps. Although we don't have wings, we hunt and sting and live in nests just like them.

We hunt on our own, tracking other insects like a spy. When the moment is right, quick-as-a-flash, we scuttle forward to bite our victim and bend our backs to inflict our sting. Our stings are very powerful and the venom acts quickly to paralyze our prey.

Gripping tightly, we carry our victim between our long mandibles back to our nest. It can be seven times as heavy as us. The insect is chewed up and fed to the larvae. They are the meat-eaters.

Our colony only has about a 1,000 ants, so we all work hard to find enough food. When the colony is small, even our queen takes care of the eggs and her larvae, and goes out of the nest to hunt.

We all protect our nest from attack. When we are annoyed we leap around. We also chase after invaders, such as spiders and cockroaches to scare them off and get them away from our nest.

Other ants are our fiercest enemies. Although they are much smaller than we are, they can overwhelm us with their great numbers. But we don't give up easily. Even if our bodies are split in half, our heads continue to bite and our tails lash out to sting.

Like all ants, we fight for the survival of our colony, fearlessly facing death. ❖

# Glossary

**Allergic reaction**
A very sensitive body reaction when something is eaten, touched, breathed in, or injected.

**Antennae**
Moveable parts on an insect's head that pick up senses.

**Bivouac**
An army ants' nest created by linking together their own bodies. [The term also means an army camp that is set up for a short time.]

**Colony**
A group of ants that live together.

**Compost**
A pile of rotting plants and animals that becomes fine soil that is full of nutrients.

**Fungus**
A plant-like living thing, such as a toadstool or mould, that does not make its own food, but lives on decaying plants and animals.

**Honeydew**
A sweet sticky liquid that oozes out of aphids and other small scaly insects.

**Larva**
The newly hatched legless form of an ant.

**Mandibles**
The mouthparts of an insect used for grabbing, biting, cutting, and chewing food.

**Paralyze**
To make an animal unable to move.

**Prey**
An animal hunted or captured for food.

**Queen ant**
A female ant that lays the eggs.

**Raid**
A surprise sudden attack by an army.

**Regurgitate**
To bring food that has been swallowed back up again into the mouth.

**Soldier ant**
The largest ants of the colony that protect the worker ants and defend the nest from intruders.

**Stinger**
A sharp-pointed tip of an ant's abdomen that can prick a victim and inject venom.

**Swarm**
A large number of flying insects.

**Tropical**
An area where the climate is hot and humid all year around.

**Venom**
A poisonous liquid that some ants inject into their victim by stinging.

**Worker ant**
The smaller ants of the colony that look after the queen, the eggs, and larvae, dig out the chambers of the nest, and forage for food.

# Index